CLOSE CALL

Anita "Nikki" Gibbs

Close Call

Dedication

[5]

I would like to thank God for everything in my life. It's wonderful to wake up knowing that He has given me a second chance to get it right.

TABLE OF CONTENTS

Foreword

When you cross paths with a girl who's faced tough times but still carries a big, open heart, it's like stumbling upon a rare gem. Her love has the power to transform you, opening your eyes to true love, self-love, and a zest for life. Despite the challenges she's endured, her resilience shines through, highlighting the depth of her character. She's a blend of elegance and a touch of street-smart, a force to be reckoned with but also a beacon of compassion. To have her as a friend is a blessing, but to mistreat her would be a mistake you'd regret. It's in how you treat her that you'll see the different facets of her personality. Cherish her, for she knows the pain of battles and the joy of triumphs. Her scars speak of courage found in vulnerability and stories of strength. Her love is a precious gift she willingly shares with those she holds dear. So, if you're lucky to have a girl like her in your life, honor her journey, stand by her side, and cherish her for the rare treasure she is.

CHAPTER ONE

Journey to Senegal

"Mademoiselle!"

"Mademoiselle!"

"Bonjour."

I'd reply. "Bonjour, Como se va?" Tickled pink, I'd just smile and continue my crossword puzzle. I was on Delta Airlines headed for the Motherland, Africa. "Mademoiselle!" The small boy kept calling me. His dad kept pulling his shirt so that he would leave me alone. He tried getting my attention the entire flight. I smiled under my mask.

Once I arrived, everything was moving at a fast pace. Being in Senegal was quite interesting. My first impression, it was a mixture of South Korea and Tijuana. I guess every country has their low points. Nothing is wrong with South Korea or Tijuana, both had beautiful sceneries. I had some great moments in Korea.

I stayed at the Djily Mbaye, an apartment in Dakar city. The establishment was two minutes from Beceao beach in Dakar Yoff. The rooms were very nice and, of course, had internet access and flat screens. There was a large kitchen and living room available. Every morning fresh croissants were delivered from the local bakery. The rooms, furniture, and the style of the bathrooms looked elegant. Although things looked pretty, strange bugs were flying all around. Of course I complained, I hate all bugs!

The concierge told me "Welcome to Africa." I really had to laugh to myself. I should have known things would be a lot different there. "Hell, I am not in the Army anymore. I could complain, I had choices!" I had a lovely time considering, and the staff were amazing. In comparison to San Diego, my visit to Senegal was not expensive at all. It was interesting that the staff did my laundry for me. It was great there as time progressed. There was so much to see and do. Senegal has many beautiful customs. It has been considered a cultural mecca of the African continent. The women wore beautiful swatches of bright cloth, and the men wore brilliant colors and skullcaps.

One thing for sure, I did not have to search far for a beach. They were extremely crowded. Whoa, people were jogging, walking, and children playing. I walked around a lot. There were little huts set up for relaxing and people gathered to take pictures. Ugh! A variety of foods, especially meat. I did not eat much while I was there. In fact, I lost six pounds. The people said that I was picky. I couldn't understand many words, but picky I understood. LOL!!

Chez Fatou was my favorite restaurant there. I went to several restaurants and tried many gourmet meals. Good thing that I liked rice, grilled chicken, and fish. I will say the fish was the yummiest. Also, found a place that serves grilled chicken tacos.

The people treated me so kindly. I felt like royalty most days. I guess they were being kind because they knew I was visiting. Once they learned that I was from the United States, they had a lot of questions. I did some touring while I was there. I went to the African Renaissance Monument in Dakar. The statue was beautiful and huge! It had so many stairs, but I enjoyed it. I was scheduled to visit the house of slaves, but there was a scheduling conflict because of the pandemic. I traveled all around Senegal seeing what all I could see. I was so excited to be there. I had some great moments being on my two-week vacation, even during a pandemic. Most people dream of going to Africa. I thank God, I made it there and back safely.

CHAPTER TWO
The Pandemic

In March, the week of our final show, "Little Rock Nine," I received the most shocking news. When I got to rehearsal, I noticed the director and manager didn't have their material. The director gathered everyone and mentioned that the next show was canceled. The college and the world were being shut down due to the spread of the Coronavirus, also known as COVID-19. We would no longer be meeting.

The pandemic took the nation by storm, affecting every aspect of life. Hospitals were overwhelmed, some forced to close their doors due to the influx of patients. Healthcare providers were risking their lives every day on the front lines, many falling ill themselves.

Nursing homes were hit hard, with the virus exposing the vulnerabilities in the long-term care system. Families struggled financially, many facing job losses and food shortages.

Grocery store shelves were often bare, with essential items like water and cleaning supplies in high demand.

Stay-at-home orders were issued, businesses closed, and schools shifted to remote learning. Masks became a mandatory accessory, and social distancing became the new norm. The world had changed overnight, and uncertainty loomed in the air. As the months passed, vaccines became available, offering a glimmer of hope. However, skepticism and fear lingered, preventing some from getting vaccinated. The world slowly adapted to a new way of living, but the scars left by the pandemic ran deep.

As the years went by, COVID-19 remained a threat, affecting lives and livelihoods. The job market took a hit, plunging the country into a recession. Unemployment rates soared, leaving many struggling to make ends meet.

The severity of the virus was immense, with the respiratory illness causing widespread damage to the lungs. The public was urged to take precautions, especially older Americans who were more vulnerable to the virus.

In 2024, the President himself tested positive for COVID-19, underscoring the ongoing battle against the virus. The CDC continued to advise individuals to stay home if sick, highlighting the importance of protecting oneself and others.

The pandemic had reshaped society in ways no one could have predicted. It taught us resilience, compassion, and the value of human connection. As we looked towards a future still marred by uncertainty, one thing remained certain – the world would never be the same again.

CHAPTER THREE
Close Calls

It was a whirlwind of events leading up to my fiftieth birthday. A day filled with celebrations and unexpected twists. Little did I know, close calls seemed to follow me like a shadow. In 2024, on the day I was scheduled to fly to San Diego, a sudden tornado disrupted our serene evening. Hail the size of softballs bombarded us as we sat helplessly in the SUV. The wind howled, trees swayed, and fear gripped my heart. But amidst the chaos, my guy's calm demeanor reassured me. We huddled in the backseat, waiting for the storm to pass, grateful to emerge unscathed from nature's fury.

Flashback to 2020, a year marked by challenges and prayers for guidance. A fateful car accident on the freeway shook me to the core. The impact was jarring, the aftermath chaotic. Struggling to regain composure, I found myself amidst a sea of horns blaring, lights flashing, and voices calling out. Miraculously, an off-duty cop became my guardian angel, guiding me to safety as my car lay mangled, a casualty of the collision.

Then, in 2018, a casual evening turned into a nightmare as my convertible met its end at the hands of an uninsured driver. The police's lackluster response left me stranded, grappling with the aftermath alone. Walking away from the wreckage, I couldn't help but ponder the series of near-misses that had punctuated my life in recent years.

Through it all, I found solace in faith, resilience in the face of adversity, and a renewed appreciation for life's fragility. As I reflect on these close calls, I am reminded of the fragility of our existence and the unpredictable nature of fate. Each encounter with danger served as a stark reminder to cherish every moment and embrace each day as a precious gift. And so, I march forward, carrying the lessons of the past as guiding beacons into an uncertain future.

A Series of Unfortunate Events

Two days before my wedding in 2008, I decided to take a casual ride on my Suzuki TL 1000R, feeling invincible. Dressed in croc shoes, jeans, and no protective gear, I set out for a quick trip to the store. Little did I know, it would be anything but normal.

As I navigated the road, a reckless driver in a gray truck carelessly ran me off the road. I was thrown off my motorcycle, landing in a heap of torn clothing and bloody injuries. My body was a canvas of pain, but miraculously, my face remained unscathed. Was this a sign from a higher power, cautioning me about my impending marriage?

Fast forward to 2005, where my streak of unfortunate events continued. Despite raising concerns about my UPS truck, I was assured that everything was fine. However, fate had other plans. While driving down Pleasant Rd, near Black & Decker Inc., my worst fear materialized - my brakes failed.

Panicked and desperate for help, I found myself dangling from my seatbelt, the truck precariously lodged in a ditch. Despite sustaining injuries, including a thigh contusion and knee damage, I felt a strange sense of protection, as if a divine force was watching over me.

In 2004, during my favorite month of April, a birthday celebration turned into a nightmare. A loud bang echoed through the air as my car collided with another vehicle, leaving me in a state of detachment. I felt disconnected from my body as I was airlifted to Carolina Medical Center, unsure of my fate.

Battling tremors and confusion, I found myself on the brink of life and death. Yet, with sheer determination, I emerged from the ordeal, greeted by concerned loved ones at the hospital. As I walked out that night, with clouds parting above, I couldn't help but feel a sense of gratitude for surviving against all odds.

Through these harrowing experiences, I learned that life's twists and turns can test us in unimaginable ways, but it is our resilience and faith that guide us through the darkest of times.

In the year 1997, I found myself stationed in Fort Bragg, North Carolina, in a signal unit where we proudly donned berets as part of our impressive uniforms. These soft caps may have added a touch of elegance to our appearance, but they offered little protection when it truly mattered.

One fateful morning, as I diligently went about my duties in the motor pool, tragedy struck. I was atop a 5-ton truck, preparing for a field assignment, when a careless oversight led to a harrowing fall. Unbeknownst to me, the tailgate I was standing on was not properly secured. In a split second, I plummeted to the ground below.

Thankfully, the tailgate did not collide with me, but I was not as fortunate. The impact of the fall caused me to strike my head on the unforgiving pavement, rendering me unconscious. Time became a blur, and it remains a mystery to me how long I lay in that state before being discovered by my comrades and squad leader.

To my dismay, instead of being immediately taken to the Troop Medical Center for a thorough examination, I was whisked away to continue working in the field. Despite my protests of a pounding migraine, my concerns fell on deaf ears. It wasn't until darkness enveloped the sky that someone finally intervened and decided it was time for me to see a doctor.

As the days turned into weeks and the weeks into months, the repercussions of that fall became apparent. Persistent headaches became an unwelcome companion, a daily reminder of that fateful incident. I soldiered on as best I could, but I knew deep down that I was not the same person I once was.

The echoes of that day in 1997 still reverberate in my life, a constant reminder of the fragility of our existence and the importance of proper care in times of need. Though the physical wounds may have healed, the invisible scars remain, a testament to a moment that forever altered the trajectory of my journey.

CHAPTER FOUR

The No Shoulders

Deceitful Snakes in the Ground

Ah, what a lovely memory of playing in your grandmother's yard surrounded by plum and pecan trees! It's amazing how these childhood memories stick with us throughout life. The innocent laughter and carefree days spent there must hold a special place in your heart. "Watch out for the No Shoulders!" - what a quirky way for your grandmother to warn you about snakes. It's funny how we only understand these things later in life, isn't it? Snakes, known as 'No Shoulders,' indeed live up to their tricky reputation. Likewise, deceitful people, similar to snakes, can be recognized by their traits like excessive bragging, defensiveness, and avoidance of apologies. It's crucial to be wary of individuals displaying such characteristics and to protect yourself from their harmful intentions. Remember, genuine connections are worth the wait, and it's better to avoid those who bring negativity into your life.

~The Drummer~

A conversation on the phone led to a love affair, as funny as it may sound. Love, my ***! I was talking with my cousin K. T. when I heard the drum roll. He kept talking about how attractive my voice was and wanted to meet me. That day kindled something between us. We talked for over six hours that day and more that night.

We conversed for weeks before our first meeting. Our first date was his daughter's hockey game. We cruised to the game on a slingshot. It was one of my best dates ever. The time we shared that night was priceless - the laughs and songs while in the slingshot. At the end of the night, there was a tender kiss, and I shivered like the light skinned girl on Five Heartbeats.

For months, I thought he had finally found me, but things started to change. He wasn't as available, and his actions towards me shifted. Unfortunately, he turned out to be a narcissist, seeking attention and lacking empathy.

Despite the disappointment, I learned a valuable lesson. Not everything that glitters is gold, and sometimes, God's plan for us does not involve certain individuals. I prayed for guidance, and God showed me the way.

~The Welder~

I couldn't believe what was happening. The welder, a friend from my church, had asked me for help when I was in San Diego. Despite my initial hesitation, I decided to send him some money via cashapp, trusting that he would pay me back as promised.

Upon my return to South Carolina, I reached out to the welder to inquire about the repayment. His response was vague, promising to send the money soon. As I sat in church on a

Sunday morning, sharing my own struggles and hardships with the congregation, little did I know that another hardship was on its way.

When I finally confronted the welder about the money, he not only refused to repay me but also hurled insults and curses my way. Feeling betrayed and hurt, I turned to prayer for guidance and strength to overcome this unjust situation. The welder cut off all contact with me, blocking me from all forms of communication.

Months turned into a year, and I decided to make one last attempt to reconcile with the welder. As he visited my aunt's house, I hoped that this would be the moment he would do the right thing. Instead, he boasted about his newfound blessings, flaunting his material possessions without any intention of repaying me.

With a heavy heart, I confronted him and bid him farewell, refusing to be taken advantage of any longer. It was a painful lesson learned about trust and deception, teaching me to be cautious of those who seek to exploit kindness for personal gain.

~The Cadillac Man~

In a world where uncertainty lurked around every corner, a young woman found herself pondering the complexities of modern dating. Was it better to pursue the man who embodied decency, orderliness, and faith, or to be drawn to the allure of someone charming yet flawed, immersed in worldly pleasures? This internal conflict gnawed at her, leaving her torn between what she desired and what she believed was right.

As she navigated through the maze of relationships, a figure emerged - the Cadillac Man. He exuded an air of mystery, a blend of classic charm with a modern twist. Their initial encounter was like a scene from a movie, with sparks igniting between them that seemed to transcend mere physical attraction.

Their connection deepened rapidly, forming a bond that felt both emotional and spiritual. They became inseparable, sharing laughter, inside jokes, and a mutual understanding that seemed to defy explanation. It was a partnership filled with joy, adventure, and an abundance of love.

However, not all stories have a happy ending. As jealousy reared its ugly head in the form of a she-wolf, their once harmonious relationship began to crumble. The challenges they faced tested the strength of their bond, eventually leading to a heartbreaking conclusion that left them both shattered.

Despite the pain of their parting, the memories of their time together remained etched in their hearts. The Cadillac Man had left an indelible mark on her soul, a reminder that sometimes, even the most beautiful stories can end in tragedy. And so, as she reflected on their journey, she realized that the Cadillac Man would forever hold a special place in her memories, a bittersweet reminder of a love that was both fleeting and eternal.

Love recognizes no barriers-- Maya Angelou

To Be or Not to Be

In the kingdom of Denmark, a young prince named Hamlet found himself trapped in the conundrum of existence. His mind tormented with the eternal question - to be or not to be.

Hamlet pondered, unsure of whether to face the adversities of life or to succumb to the unknown abyss of death. Should he endure the hardships and injustices that fate bestowed upon him, or should he rise against the tumultuous sea of troubles? The prince grappled with the notion that perhaps it would be easier to end it all, to take up arms against his oppressive reality and usher in a swift resolution. Yet, the fear of the unknown, the uncertainty of what lies beyond the veil of mortality, held him back. The undiscovered country from whose borne no traveler returns haunted his thoughts, making him hesitant to embrace death's embrace.

He mused on the struggles of life, the injustices endured, the delays in justice, and the burdens of responsibility. The weight of these tribulations bore down upon him, stifling his will and suffocating his resolve.

But in the depths of his contemplation, Hamlet realized that it was not death that frightened him, but the uncertainty of what awaited him in the afterlife. The fear of the unknown made cowards of us all, he thought, as he grappled with the paralyzing effect of conscience.

As the pale cast of thought enveloped his mind, Hamlet understood that true courage lay not in the acceptance of fate but in the defiance of it. With a newfound resolve, he embraced the uncertainties of life, ready to face whatever challenges may come his way.

And thus, the prince of Denmark set forth on a path of self-discovery, armored not with the fear of death but with the courage to navigate the turbulent waters of existence. In that moment of clarity, Hamlet found the strength to choose to be, to confront life's trials head-on, and to carve his own destiny in the face of adversity.

CHAPTER FIVE
Agony Vs. Anger

No one has ever thought to ask me how It felt to be me. Most just want whatever there is that I can give them. The fact that I have taken such a devastating blow from this journey of Life means nothing to anyone.

Guess you never know who you are or who's you are until something serious happens to you. Here I was thinking that I was important to so many because of my good deeds. I once heard that if you do good things that good comes back to you. Nope! That was not my case. I can count on six fingers those who were there for me, laugh out loud. I thank God for them.

AGONY Like Never Before

I experienced whiplash; not being able to move my neck (stiff neck). I could not use a pillow for months. I just laid my face on the bed while sleeping on my stomach. I had difficulty focusing, extreme headaches and a sensation of pins and needles down my spine. I had tenderness to the left shoulder because I was slammed into the car door. There was some numbness in my left arm. My face was swollen and red. I experienced many days and nights of fatigue, dizziness, numbness, and sleep disorder. Of course, I had on my seat belt. The airbag did not deploy. There was sharp, stabbing pain shooting down my legs some days and other days numbness. One day I was sure that I was paralyzed. Often, I'd feel pain in my lower back and hip like a crucifixion as if nails were going into my flesh and separating my bones. This pain hindered me from moving around or walking.

ANGER Had A Hold Of Me

I deleted, unfriended, or blocked people who did not help. If I ever done anything for you, and you turned your back on me to hell with you. I was angry because they knew my situation yet did not offer a helping hand. I asked for help and was still turned down. People really showed me who they were. I was disappointed in my so-called friends and family that called me to be nosy. Yes, if you called to ask about my condition and you lived in my city, you were just being Dang nosy! I was honest whenever someone asked how I was feeling. I was in a tremendous amount of pain. Although I was alone and in excruciating pain, I praised God for my life. Even though my legs and arms didn't work every day, I was glad to have them. I limped some days singing my favorite song, "You don't know like I know what He's done for me!"

The Night Before Flight

My holiday trip was planned out to the tee. I mean I was Rhett to go! Twas' the night before the flight I was drinking my cider. Not a creature was stirring, not even a spider. I began prepping for my holiday trip. While bathing, I was singing an old familiar tune. "Dun, dun, dun, I'm dreaming of a white Christmas." I heard a loud BANG! The heat shut off, the lights became dim, and one blew out. "Dammit! Dammit! I yelled, and suddenly there was a blackout. I turned the water off, got out of the shower, grabbed a tower and headed toward the balcony. Yep! The entire neighborhood was dark. Bumping into everything in my path, I was able to get a candle and lighter. Woo Hoo! Hmm, I thought about my Uber ride and all Surprisingly, I did not panic. I got dressed, fixed something to eat and laid on the bed.

On my phone I began to watch BET, the Black entertainment channel. As I was watching Sisters, I thought about my phone wasn't going to be charged so I shut that down. I set several alarms and scheduled a wakeup call with Carmela, my sister. I didn't get a wink of sleep! Too afraid I'd miss my flight. Lol! It was the Army all over again. Instead of a canteen to bathe, I used the cold faucet and body wash. I had to put my phone's flashlight against the mirror to wash my face and brush my teeth. "God help me, " I screamed while trying to draw my eyebrows. I felt like Anna Mae Bullock. I had enough of that stuff. I should have drawn a straight line like most women.

I made dang sure my clothes were on properly with tags in the right place. Oh boy! I was finally dressed and ready. I summoned my Uber to come. Smh (shaking my head)! I could barely see the steps. My bags kept falling, but I remained calm. I had the phone's flashlight on, but it was so freaking dark out. I thought about NTC, national training center while in the Army. I could do this, I said to myself.

I waited patiently for the Uber on the dark, lonely and cold sidewalk. I held my phone in the air so the driver could see me. So glad I had the experience in the military. I was able to get dressed by candlelight and be presentable. I did not complain. I am Army strong!

If the Walls Could Talk

In the midst of chaos and pain, I found myself in a dark place both physically and emotionally. Each day was a battle against my own body, a struggle that seemed never-ending. The walls of my room witnessed my outbursts, my screams filled with anger and frustration. I lashed out at anyone and everyone, searching for someone to share the burden of my suffering.

Some days, I would find myself on the floor, overwhelmed by the weight of my pain, questioning why I was forced to endure such agony alone. The world outside carried on, oblivious to the turmoil within me. I felt abandoned, lost in a sea of despair. As the rain poured outside, mirroring the storm raging inside me, I prepared to leave for yet another chiropractor appointment. But a simple message from my Aunt Jean, a song reminding me that God's blessings were still upon me, brought me to my knees in gratitude.

In that moment of despair, when I felt like all hope was lost, a flicker of light shone through the darkness. I was reminded of the words, "If God brings you to it, He will bring you through it." And though I was far from feeling optimistic, I clung to the belief that God's plan for me was not yet finished.

With tear-stained cheeks and a heart heavy with doubt, I cried out to the heavens, seeking solace in the promise of divine assistance. In my weakness, I found strength in knowing that God would see me through, His unwavering love a beacon of hope in my darkest hour.

And so, I rose from the depths of despair, renewed in faith and gratitude. Though the road ahead was fraught with challenges, I faced it with the knowledge that I was not alone. With

God by my side, I would overcome, no matter how difficult the journey may be.

In the depths of darkness, amidst the choir's melodic voices filling the church with hope, Mr. Elmore's rendition of Job's trials echoed in my soul. His powerful voice struck a chord within me, questioning why suffering had to befall us. The pain I endured seemed endless, the unrelenting burden of sickness weighing me down.

As days turned into months, my struggle became a constant companion. Simple tasks became monumental challenges, and the outside world blurred into a distant memory. The reliance on Uber rides and food deliveries highlighted my isolation, my existence reduced to mere survival. Yet, in the midst of despair, a flicker of faith burned within me. Despite the darkness enveloping my life, I clung to the belief that my suffering had a purpose. Pastor Rickey's words resonated in my mind, urging me to pray until something happened, to persevere in the face of adversity.

Days turned into weeks, and weeks into months. Tears mingled with prayers as I navigated the shadows that threatened to consume me. Each day brought its own battles, but I refused to succumb to despair. The darkness that surrounded me served as a reminder that even in the bleakest moments, a glimmer of light could emerge.

Finally, after months of anguish and uncertainty, I saw a ray of sunlight piercing through the darkness. It was a gradual awakening, a slow realization that my faith had sustained me through the storm. The journey through darkness had led me to a newfound appreciation for the light, a profound understanding that even in the deepest shadows, hope still prevailed.

The Nine

I am healing day by day with God's help. I hold in a lot. When I'm in pain, I don't like to worry other people. No matter how much somebody asks, my answer is always," I am fine," even if it's not true. I am not a numbers lady, but I know that every number has a meaning. The number nine symbolizes divine completeness. It also represents the fruits of God's Holy Spirit.

After the long bickering, cussing, fussing, and praying, some things changed. There were nine Angels that appeared. I must say that a few of them were a total surprise. I thank God for them all. Prayer works!

The City Manager

Oh wow, Mrs. DT! She is one dedicated, hardworking, and strong woman. She'd do whatever she could for me. She had a full-time job working in management in her department. Also, being a mom with a Navy sailor on deployment. DT cooked Thanksgiving dinner too, I did what I could. I could not stand much, and I had to sit with pillows. The children made me feel as comfortable as possible. Mrs. DT made sure that I was not alone on the holiday. I had a wonderful time with them.

Houston Couple

Now, this was an extreme pleasure. The Adams (Mr. C & Mrs. S) family came all the way from Houston to check on me. They used to attend my old church in La Mesa. I was so thrilled to see them that a tear dropped my eye. This loving couple brought me groceries and a beautiful plant. It was so wonderful seeing the family. We had lunch and a great conversation. They really made my day. God bless them.

MLK Singer

Oh yeah, Miss Kay from the MLK choir. Although she was grumpy about the pandemic, she delivered groceries to me. She made a quick appearance, and I gave her a thank you card. I was happy that she came out despite the traumatic experience of the Pandemic. She is such a sweet lady. I love when we sing next to each other. I was so surprised that she came out.

Homemaker

Of course, every now and then, I would hear from Miss Ya. She was a member of my old church in La Mesa. She took me to a few places. We had lunch at our favorite taco shop. Miss Ya was so much fun, and I appreciated her for coming by. I thanked her for the good moments, especially the great laughs.

Mail Clerk

The kind-hearted mail clerk, Miss G. She was a member of my old church in La Mesa. She read about my car accident on Facebook. She sent me her phone number via messenger. Jesus! She told me that she refused to take no for an answer. That same evening, she and her granddaughter stopped by. God is so amazing! Not only did she bring me dinner, but she also had a Christmas gift as well. I was so happy to see the two of them. I was thrilled and full of joy to have such a wonderful gift for Christmas. Miss G has retired from the post office, and God has blessed her with a wonderful husband.

The Dancing Usher

I was truly grateful when the Usher from my old church called to help. He saw my accident on Facebook and reached out. The Dancing Usher is what we called him. He would praise and worship like no other. I thanked him for bringing food and water at such a needy time. I have been blessed with such a caring and loving friend. God bless this dancing man of God.

The Jazz singer

I appreciated Ms. D, she volunteered to take me to a few places. I asked her if she was sure because I knew it was a huge responsibility. I took people to their appointments for years. Of course, it only lasted two weeks, laugh out loud. I wasn't mad at all. That was two weeks I did not have to give money to an Uber. Ms. D continues to call and check on me from time to time.

The Dance Instructor

I was surprised when Cowboy Collins, also known as CC, offered to take me to an appointment. Hell, he was surprised that I was paying so much money for Uber. He saw my accident on Facebook. I was truly grateful for his help. It felt good knowing that others cared.

DJ-Jay

All hell broke loose one night at the American Legion. It was shut down early because of turmoil. Everyone had to leave the premises. I was having trouble with my Uber app. Aw man! I didn't need that shi!!! I asked everyone that was in my circle that night for a ride. The one that I bought food for, drinks, and gave rides too. They all told me NO! Also asked the guy, Bill, who was trying to get with me that night. He said, "No, I live up north," with a mean proper accent. I became extremely angry. As I kept trying the Uber app, security asked me to come back into the building for my safety. While sitting by the front desk, a kind and gentle man named Jay, asked me why I was still there. He asked, "What happened to your friends?" I replied, "What friends? Those f**** turned their backs on me." He asked if I needed a ride. He took me home and told me to uninstall the app and re-install it. Ha-ha. I think it stopped working so that I would stop dealing with certain people. I had been using Uber for six months without any issues. I thought I had a system. Yeah right! I was the dang system. People called me when they needed something. It felt good knowing that there are some good people in the world with a kind heart like me. So glad that I have a wonderful friend in DJ-Jay. He continues to check on me. Sounds crazy but I learned.

The Revelation of Life

In the journey of life, we often encounter moments that shake us to our core. For one woman, the hardest pill to swallow was learning that no matter how much love and kindness she poured into others, they could still turn their backs on her. This realization cut deep, affecting her relationships with family, friends, companions, and colleagues. Despite the pain, she found the strength to keep moving forward, refusing to tolerate any mistreatment. "I'd rather have genuine peace than false warmth," she thought to herself. As she grappled with this revelation, she turned to her faith, finding solace in the belief that there was a greater plan at work.

But God...

She found comfort in the idea that sometimes God asks us to release the things we hold most dear as a test of faith. Trusting in the process, she understood that God's plans may not align with hers, but they were always for her ultimate good. As she navigated the challenges of life, she reflected on the power of sisterhood. Coming together as women, supporting each other through trust, loyalty, and compassion, they created a force for positive change in the world.

Joining the Alpha Alpha Gamma Psi Christian Sorority, she found a sense of belonging and purpose. This sisterhood, built on the principles of love, care, and unity, provided her with a supportive community in which she could thrive.

As she embraced the journey ahead, she realized that closed doors were not disasters but divine interventions guiding her towards a greater destiny. She understood that setbacks were often setups for something greater, and she placed her trust in God's plan for her life.

In the end, she discovered that true strength came from surrendering to the will of a higher power, embracing the challenges as opportunities for growth, and

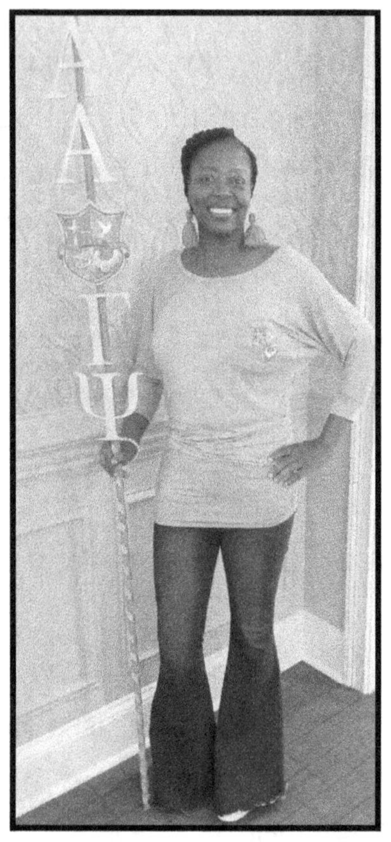

finding solace in the unbreakable bond of sisterhood. And so, she walked forward with faith in her heart, knowing that no matter what trials may come her way, she had the resilience, support, and unwavering grace to overcome.

Who Am I?

I am strong, I am brave.

Sometimes I am good.

Sometimes I misbehave.

When people see me, I'm a black spade.

Inside, I'm an exploding grenade.

I'm just a woman trying to become good.

Oftentimes, I am misunderstood.

It is not easy being me.

I have been the best that I can be.

I prayed that God send me love.

He sent his best, some loving doves.

I am who I am.

There's no one like me.

The one and only BLAZZE, AKA NIKKI

That's who I am.

N. Gibbs

~Better~

In this chapter of my life, the title is "Better." I have embraced the notion of doing better now that I know better. It's a realization that I cannot revert to the same old ways of thinking that once governed my actions. Sure, mistakes will still be made, but the beauty lies in the fact that they will be new mistakes signifying growth and progress.

My authentic self no longer seeks validation from fitting in; instead, I am paving my unique path. I am filled with the confidence that better things are on the horizon, an inevitable part of life's journey. The excitement of exploring uncharted territories fills me with a sense of purpose and joy.

Engaging in activities that bring me genuine pleasure has become my priority. Volunteering with Alpha Alpha Gamma Psi Christian Sorority, serving as the community liaison with Kingdom Group Corporation, and participating in stage plays with Hicklin Entertainment, Sheila Culp Production, and Common Ground Theatre in San Diego are just a few chapters of my rich and vibrant life story. Furthermore, my involvement as an active member of the American Legion Post 34 adds a sense of community and camaraderie to my days. As I revel in my well-deserved retirement, I am grateful for the opportunities that come my way, crafting an exciting and fulfilling life that I wholeheartedly embrace.

~Wake Up! ~

I couldn't believe what was happening around me. The blaring sirens, flashing lights, and concerned faces made me realize something terrible must have occurred. My head was throbbing, and as I tried to speak, I felt a sharp pain in my mouth. Confusion clouded my mind until a voice broke through, "Ma'am, are you okay? Are you all right?" "Huh," was all I could manage to reply. The memories started flooding back - a sudden impact, screeching tires, and then darkness. I touched my face and felt a dull ache, realizing I was wearing a mask. Panic set in as I wondered if my teeth were broken.

The next thing I knew, I was being carefully placed on a gurney by paramedics. The scene around me was chaotic, with firefighters, police officers, and a crowd of onlookers buzzing with questions and concerns.

"You were in an accident. An eighteen-wheeler hit you from behind and fled the scene," a reassuring police officer informed me. He mentioned that they had cameras at every exit and assured me that they would track down the culprit.

At the hospital, doctors confirmed I had suffered minor injuries and released me later that night. As I sat in the quiet of my hospital room, the gravity of what had occurred started to sink in. I was grateful to be alive but shaken by the close call. The events of that day would forever serve as a reminder of the fragility of life and the importance of cherishing each waking moment.

Mahogany's Mind

The Other Side

In a realm of love's allure,

Where once I felt secure,

A shadow's touch, a bitter

sting,

A twisted tale I now must sing.

At first, a charmer's guise you

wore,

With gentle words and heart's allure.

Your calls brought solace to my soul,

Your invitations made me whole.

But like a serpent's cloak, your guise did shed,

Revealing a darkness I should have fled.

The texts that once were filled with grace,

Now echo with a cruel embrace.

From loving whispers to a deafening roar,

Your words now pierce me to the core.

Screams and shouts, a desperate plea,

To reach the heart you've stolen from me.
The love we shared, a twisted game,
A mockery of its former flame.
Now, in the wreckage of our shattered dreams,
I'm left with wounds and broken seams.

But though your words may sting and burn,
My heart will heal, my spirit will yearn.
For in the depths of this cruel despair,
I'll find the strength to break
free from your snare.

No more will I be held captive by your spell,
No more will I allow your words to dwell.
For I am worthy of love that's true,
A love that will uplift and renew.
So, let your texts continue to rage,
Your venom will no longer engage.
For I have risen from the ashes of your scorn,
A phoenix reborn, my spirit reborn.
A. N. Gibbs

Miss You

In the realm of longing,

where absence reigns,

I yearn for your touch,

a solace that sustains.

Each moment apart

feels like an eternity,

A void that echoes with a solitude

that sets me free.

Your gentle caress,

a balm for my weary soul,

A spark that ignites a flame

that makes me whole.

Your fingers tracing patterns on my skin,

A symphony of sensations

that sets my heart akin.

Through the darkness, I cling to the memory of

your touch,

A beacon of hope that keeps

me going so much.

I'll endure the loneliness, the emptiness I feel,

Knowing that one day,

I'll hold you close and heal.

Till then, my dreams shall be

a sanctuary of delight,

Where your touch envelops me,

making everything right.

I'll close my eyes and imagine your embrace,

A comforting haven where

I find solace and grace.

For in the tapestry of love,

your touch is the thread,

That binds our hearts together,

leaving me never to dread.

So I'll wait patiently, with hope in my breast,

Until the day I'm home with you,

and my soul finds rest.

A. N. Gibbs

One

One Touch

One touch, a spark ignites within,

A flame that burns, a love I'll spin.

How much could it mean, this simple caress,

A promise of bliss, a path to bless?

One look, a window to your soul,

Depths I've never seen, a captivating toll.

Your eyes, a mirror reflecting my own,

Revealing the love that's destined to be known.

One smile, a beacon in the night,

Guiding me through darkness,

making me feel right.

I've loved it for a while, a secret I've kept,

But now I'll confess, my heart cannot be slept.

One love, sent from heaven above,

A gift I'll cherish, a treasure I'll shove.

With every touch, look, and smile,

My love for you grows, reaching a mile.

A. N. Gibbs

Your Voice

Your Voice, My Solace

At day's end, your voice, a soothing balm,
Calms my soul and brings me endless calm.
Like a gentle breeze, it whispers sweet,
Assuring me that all is well, complete.

Your words, a symphony to my ear,
Ease my worries and banish every fear.
Your laughter fills me with pure delight,
A precious gift that makes my world so bright.

When darkness falls and shadows dance,
Your voice becomes my guiding light, my
chance.
It leads me through the night's uncertain maze,
To a place where love and peace eternally

graze.

Your love, a haven where I find my rest,
A sanctuary where my heart is truly blessed.
It's all I need to face life's every test,
For with your love, I am forever blessed.

So let your voice forever grace my ear,
A timeless melody that eases every care.
Your voice, my solace, my eternal guide,
A love so deep, it's my unwavering pride.

At Last

A Love's Embrace

When our eyes meet, a spark ignites,

Our lips entwined, a symphony of delights.

Oh, how my heart beats with love's sweet fire,

As your embrace fills me with pure desire.

Your tender touch, a balm upon my soul,

Your warm embrace, a haven where I'm whole.

Finally, face to face, our dreams come true,

United in a love that forever shall pursue.

Your arms enfold me, a fortress strong,

Protecting me from all that could go wrong.

God, this feels so right, so meant to be,

A love so deep, it sets my spirit free.

Our hearts race with anticipation's thrill,

As we anticipate the passion we will fulfill.

Together at last, our souls entwined,

A love so rare, a treasure we will find.

A. N. Gibbs

First Sight

In the twilight's embrace, our eyes met,

A spark ignited, a love we'd not yet.

At first sight, my heart danced with delight,

In the presence of a soul so pure and bright.

Though our laughter filled the air that night,

We held back,

knowing the line we dared not cross.

For in that moment, we sought not a kiss,

But a connection deeper, a love that would last.

We shared our thoughts and dreams, our

hopes and fears,

Discovering the harmony we held so dear.

With every word, the bond between us grew,

A tapestry of love, so vibrant and true.

We drew a line, a boundary we'd not break,

Preserving the sanctity

of love we wished to make.

In that night's embrace, we found our way,

A love built on trust, a love that would stay.

A. N. Gibbs

Home

Carolina's Embrace

From Carolina's verdant hills I strayed,

To return again, my heart betrayed.

Into the arms of one I held so dear,

My dearest friend, my love so clear.

With trembling voice, I shared my plight,

That I must leave, embark on a new flight.

He met my gaze, his eyes filled with pain,

'Can I persuade you, love, to still remain?'

The date escapes my mind, a fading trace,

But in my soul, I knew it was fate's embrace.

Our friendship's bond, a sacred tie,

For him, I'd gladly climb mountains high.

His love I cherish, a precious flame,

With him beside me, life is never tame.

In his embrace, I find solace and grace,

Carolina's love, an eternal embrace.

A. N. Gibbs

The Last Time

In distant realms, where memories reside,
A tale of love, once shattered, I confide.
For long, I roamed, my heart astray,

His touch forgotten, a distant way.
With heartfelt pleas, he begged me to return,
His words like echoes, my spirit to burn.
He claimed to miss me, his love so strong,
But once, I was a token, left alone and wrong.
On a shelf he placed me, my value concealed,
My heart in pieces, his actions revealed.

The damage wrought, too deep to mend,
I bid him farewell, my journey to end.
'Take care, my friend,' I whispered low,
A final farewell, a painful blow.
No more could I endure the endless pain,
My mind resolved, I walked out again.
This time, it was final, my heart set free,

No more would I be bound, no more decree.

I followed my path, my spirit renewed,

Leaving behind the love that once subdued.

A. N. Gibbs

A Thought

In slumber's embrace, your image appears,

A sweet reverie that banishes fears.

Your whispered words, a symphony to my ears,

Proclaiming me yours, erasing all years.

When distance separates, a void within,

A longing gnaws, a sorrow akin

To a lost soul, wandering and forlorn,

Yet your memory sustains me,

like a beacon at dawn.

Your touch, a spark that ignites my soul,

Your voice,

a melody that makes my spirit whole.

In your absence, I'm lost, adrift at sea,

But your thought alone.

sets my captive heart free.

You're the sun that brightens my every day,

The reason I smile, the love that I can't convey.

In the tapestry of life, you're my vibrant thread,

A love so profound, a bond that can't be shed.

My heart overflows with love, so pure and true,
A treasure I hold, a dream that's come through.
In your embrace, I find solace and peace,
For in your love, all my worries cease.
A. N. Gibbs

UGH!

Disregard My Mind

Disregard my mind, it races wild,

Anxious thoughts, a restless child.

My feet keep pacing, to and fro,

Mesmerized by your charm, I glow.

I belong in your arms, my love,

Where peace resides, like a white dove.

I know that all will be serene,

Once I cross that county line, unseen.

Though unsure of what lies ahead,

I trust you, my heart's guiding thread.

Your love envelops me like a cloak,

Shielding me from doubt's heavy yoke.

So disregard my mind's anxious plea,

For in your embrace, I'll be set free.

Your love's embrace, a beacon bright,

Dispels the darkness, filling me with light.

A. N. Gibbs

[71]

Once Loved

Love's Shadow

Light turned to darkness, a sudden eclipse,

Sunlight drowned in rain, a cruel twist.

The one I cherished, now a source of pain,

My heart shattered, a fractured refrain.

Lies whispered sweet, like poison's caress,

'You're the love of my life,' a hollow jest.

Now deceit's venom courses through my veins,

Torture and strife, an endless refrain.

Torn apart, I wander in a haze,

Lost and broken, consumed by a maze.

He failed to see the depths of my plight,

His actions shattered my heart's delicate light.

Oh, cruel love, a twisted, bitter game,

Where light and hope are

extinguished in shame.

I am left in darkness, adrift and alone,

Haunted by memories that cut like a stone.

A. N. Gibbs

Broken

The Broken Heart's Lament

In the crash of shattered dreams,

Where love's flame burns and screams,

I'm lost in a void of pain,

A heart forever torn in twain.

Yearning for what can never be,

Hope flickers dimly, setting me free,

But dreams lie shattered, bittersweet,

A haunting reminder of what I'll never meet.

The pains that pierce, the stings that sting,

A symphony of sorrow that I can't unring,

A broken heart bleeds its every tear,

As memories torment me, filling me with fear.

In the depths of despair, I'm torn apart,

My broken heart, a shattered work of art,

Yearning for a love that's lost and gone,

A soul forever wounded, left to mourn.

.

A. N. Gibbs

[73]

Nervous

Unspoken Love

In whispers I yearn, my heart ablaze,

But silence muffles, obscuring my gaze.

I fall deeper, adrift in a sea,

While you, my love, remain distant and free.

Your presence ignites a fire in my soul,

My heart races, as if at a goal.

I tremble with nerves, a fluttering flight,

Longing to embrace you in the pale moonlight.

Though weeks may divide, a month soon pass,

My love for you burns, a radiant mass.

I cannot fathom the reason or why,

But your love consumes me,

beneath the vast sky.

My heartstrings tug, a melody untold,

A symphony of emotions, forever bold.

All I know, my darling, is clear and true,

My love for you, forever pure and new.

A. N. Gibbs

Time

My Heart's Delight

In these past months, a sweet embrace,

Your presence fills my heart with grace.

At the mere thought of you,

my pulse takes flight,

My soul ignited by your loving light.

Calls, hangouts, texts, a symphony of bliss,

Each moment shared, a precious kiss.

The future holds wonders, yet to be known,

But with you by my side, I'll never roam.

In times of stress, your touch brings calm,

Releasing tension, like a soothing balm.

Cuddles shared, a sanctuary of love,

Where worries fade, dreams take flight above.

Years have passed, our bond unyielding,

A testament to the love we're wielding.

I could sing your praises, day and night,

For you, my soulmate, my heart's true light.

Thank you, my love, for all you've given,
Making my dreams a reality, heaven-driven.
From mountaintops, I'll declare my love,
You're the one I cherish, the star above.
A. N. Gibbs

With God

A Wakeful Dream

Upon my bed, with hope astray,

I lie and wait, a nurse's sway.

A sudden chill, a pain so deep,

My body fails, my spirit weeps.

I gaze aloft, my vision dim,

This wretched state, a cruel whim.

My thoughts race wild, a frantic flight,

How shall I leave this endless night?

My kin's faces, etched with dread,

Their eyes convey the words unsaid.

My life unfolds, a fleeting scene,

A flash of light, a glimpse serene.

Then, darkness falls, a welcome veil,

As memories cascade, tears prevail.

'Amazing Grace,' it softly plays,

A balm upon my weary days.

My time has come, I now perceive,

With God's embrace, I shall believe.

But then, a voice, a gentle plea,

'Wake up, ma'am, you're illness free!'

My family's love, a beacon bright,

Leads me back to life's sweet light.

Healed and whole, my spirit soars,

A dream, a journey, forevermore.

But now you are home!

A. N. Gibbs

Cause

Triggers of Love

In a world where chaos reigns,

Your gentle touch brings me solace and peace.

Your kindness, a beacon in the darkest lanes,

Guiding my heart to find its release.

Like a delicate flower, you bloom,

With grace and beauty that fills my soul.

Your presence, a fragrant perfume,

That lingers long after you've taken your toll.

In the tapestry of life's intricate thread,

Your love is a vibrant, shimmering hue.

A treasure I hold close, a precious thread,

That binds our hearts together, me and you.

So let me sing your praises, my love so dear,

For the gentle soul, makes my life complete.

Your kindness, a balm that heals all fear,

Your presence,

A blessing that makes my heartbeat.

A. N. Gibbs

I Thank God

Love's Eternal Embrace

In the tapestry of time, our love unfurls,

A timeless bond

that neither fate nor world can hurl.

Today, tomorrow, forever, my heart beats true,

For in your embrace,

all my dreams come anew.

When we're together, joy fills every hour,

A symphony of laughter, a blissful flower.

No mountain's height, no valley's depth below,

Can dim the flame of love that we both know.

Like a river's flow, our love knows no bounds,

Connecting our souls,

where true happiness is found.

No obstacle too great, no distance too wide,

To keep me from your side, my love, my pride.

Our friendship's bond, a treasure I hold dear,

A foundation of trust, a love that conquers fear.

With every passing day,

my love grows stronger,

A beacon in my heart,

a love that will never falter.

So let the world behold our love's embrace,

A testament to time, an eternal grace.

For now, tomorrow, and forevermore,

My heart is yours, forever to adore.

A. N. Gibbs

Love Is

Love's True Embrace

When love's sweet words flow from my tongue,

My heart's intent is pure and strong.

Kindness guides my every thought,

For love's embrace should never be fraught.

Like sunshine, it brightens my day,

Chasing shadows and blues away.

Its warmth envelops, like a gentle flame,

Keeping me safe, no matter the game.

Patience whispers in my ear,

Guiding me through laughter and tear.

Love's constancy, a steady light,

Dispelling darkness, day and night.

I cherish our bond with all my might,

A love that's etched in my heart's sight.

Through trials and triumphs, it stands tall,

An unyielding beacon, through it all.

Though storms may rage and tempests roar,

Love's flame burns bright, forevermore.
For in its embrace, I find my peace,
A love that heals, a love that brings release.
So let us cherish this gift divine,
A love that's true, a love that's mine.
For in its depths, I find my soul's desire,
A love that sets my heart afire.
A.N. Gibbs

Change

Love's Fickle Flame

In the embers of passion's fire,

we danced with delight,

Laughter echoed through halls,

a symphony of light.

But as time's relentless tide did flow,

A shadow crept, casting a sinister glow.

Months unraveled, a tapestry of change,

The love we once shared,

now tethered by a strange range.

The man I held dear, a stranger in my sight,

His gaze distant, lost in a realm of night.

No longer did he whisper

sweet words in my ear,

His heart had wandered, leaving me in fear.

The flame that once burned

so brightly and true,

Now flickered and waned,

a painful sight to view.

Oh, cruel fate, why must it be so?
To break the bond that
once made my heart glow.
I search for answers, but none can I find,
Only the emptiness of a love left behind.
In the ashes of our shattered dreams, I stand,
Haunted by memories that
haunt my barren land.
The love we once shared, a bittersweet jest,
A reminder of a flame that's no more at its best.
A. N. Gibbs

Why?

Take It or Leave It

Take it or leave it, you say,

But why must it end this way?

Why can't we have a simple chat,

And unravel this tangled knot?

Love knows no bounds, it's true,

But it needs a spark to renew.

When lovers cease to communicate,

The flame flickers and threatens to abate.

Remember, love can vanish in a blink,

Leaving only echoes and a broken link.

Time slips away, and before we know,

We're left with regrets and an empty show.

Don't let pride or fear hold you back,

Reach out and bridge this widening crack.

For when love is gone, it leaves a void,

A haunting memory that can't be destroyed.

So take it or leave it, it's your choice,

But remember, love is a delicate voice.

If you let it slip away, you may find,

That the chance to say goodbye is left behind.

A. N. Gibbs

My Heart

In realms of love, where spirits soar,

You shine, a beacon I adore.

Your presence stirs a flame so bright,

Yet flutters my heart with every sight.

Your absence leaves me disarrayed,

A void within that cannot be swayed.

The distance may extend our plight,

But my love for you burns ever bright.

From dawn's embrace to twilight's gleam,

Your image lingers, a distant dream.

The longing in my soul knows no cease,

A constant ache that brings no peace.

Your laughter echoes in my mind,

A melody that makes my spirit find

Solace in the lonely hours of night,

Guiding me through darkness with its light.

My heartstrings pluck a tender tune,

A symphony of love that knows no moon.

Though fate may keep us worlds apart,

My devotion remains an unwavering art.

For you are special, a treasure I hold,
A love so precious, a story untold.
In the tapestry of life, you are my thread,
Weaving a bond that cannot be shed.
So let me whisper words of adoration,
A sonnet of love, a timeless oration.
May these verses reach your distant shore,
A testament to the love I have in store.
A. N. Gibbs

Love Lost

Lost Love's Embrace

Once, your smile ignited a flame,
A beacon of joy, a boundless claim.
I reveled in the warmth you bestowed,
Believing our bond would forever be owed.

'I love you,' you whispered, words so sweet,
Igniting a flame, my heart's eager beat.
I cherished those words, held them dear,
Trusting in their promise, dispelling all fear.

But now, a shadow has cast its blight,
Dimming the radiance of love's guiding light.
Your care has dwindled, leaving a void,
As if my heart's treasure has been destroyed.

The smile you once painted on my face,
Has faded into a somber trace.

[90]

Your presence, once a solace to my soul,
Now brings only pain, leaving me to toll.
I grieve for the love that once burned bright,
Now extinguished by darkness, a cruel sight.
I've lost my love, my beacon of grace,
And in its wake, only sorrow remains in this
space.
A. N. Gibbs

Goodbye

A Fleeting Dream

This isn't love, a mere illusion spun,

Release me as doves fly, free under the sun.

No more shall I be chained, my spirit yearns,

For another's embrace, where true love burns.

For long you've held me captive,

claimed my heart,

But now the chains have shattered,

it's time to depart.

Our love a facade, a mirage in the night,

A fleeting dream, fading with morning's light.

Though memories linger,

like whispers in the air,

In my dreams your presence lingers,

a haunting snare.

But I will find solace in a love that's real,

A flame that burns brightly,

a heart that I can feel.

So set me free, beloved, let me take my flight,

To seek a love that fills my soul with delight.

For in your absence, I will find my true worth,

A love that blossoms,

a love that's meant for Earth.

A. N. Gibbs

Forgive Me

Exonerate Me

In sorrow's depths, I beg your grace,

A trillion times, I'll seek your embrace.

For every fault, I'll berate my soul,

And kick myself, a penance to extol.

You, my friend, a treasure I hold dear,

Your worthiness, I fail to revere.

Our bond, a fragile gem I shattered wide,

With words that cut, I pierced our pride.

Forgive me, please, for my cruel jest,

I cherish our friendship, the very best.

Punish me, but let this end the strife,

For without you, my life would be bereft.

I was unkind to you, my dearest friend,

And now, in tears, I seek to mend.

Please forgive me, for I need you near,

My heart aches, consumed by fear.

A. N. Gibbs

Praying

Celestial Gratitude

In humble stance, we kneel and stand,

Our hearts uplifted to a sacred land.

With outstretched palms, we reach above,

To thank the One we know and love.

From life's trials, we've drawn our might,

Lessons learned in darkest night.

Through storms and strife,

we've found our way,

Guided by blessings, come what may.

For every victory, we give our praise,

And in defeat, we seek His grace.

For in the battles we have faced,

His love has drawn us to His sacred space.

We lift our heads to heaven's dome,

Thanking God for making us our home.

His blessings flow like gentle rain,

Nurturing our spirits, easing our pain.

[95]

With every prayer, we cast aside,

The evil that seeks to divide.

For in His love, we find our strength,

A fortress against all attacks and length.

So let us stand, let us kneel,

And let our gratitude reveal.

For in the presence of His grace,

We find our solace, our sacred space.

A. N. Gibbs

Life

Ups and Downs

Through life's journey, we'll face the tide,

With ups and downs, we'll ride the tide.

Smiles and frowns, a tapestry we weave,

But in our hands, the choice we leave.

When sorrows weigh us down to the ground,

Remember, love, you have the power bound.

To lift your head and face the fray,

To choose the path that leads to a brighter day.

The choice is yours, to make it what you will,

To embrace the joys, let go of the ill.

In every moment, a chance to find,

The happiness that fills the heart and mind.

So let us journey on, hand in hand,

Through ups and downs, we'll firmly stand.

With smiles and frowns, we'll navigate,
And choose together a life we celebrate.

For in the tapestry of our love's embrace,
We'll find the strength to win the race.
Ups and downs, we'll weather every storm,
And make our love a haven, warm and strong.
A. N. Gibbs

 Courage

Courage to Depart

I step aside, with heart ablaze,

From love unclaimed, a torturous maze.

Though tears may fall, I know it's true,

I have the strength to walk away from you.

You hold me close, yet keep me at bay,

A constant dance that leaves me in dismay.

Your words ignite a spark, but then it fades,

As I'm left yearning for what never pervades.

I've poured my soul into this empty void,

But now I see, it's time to be deployed.

I have the wisdom to discern the truth,

That I deserve a love that's pure and uncouth.

Though it may pain, I'll turn away,

From the illusion that I've tried to sway.

[99]

I'll find a love that's worthy of my all,

Where I'm cherished, valued,

and won't ever fall.

So, with a heavy heart and tear-stained face,

I bid farewell to this love's empty space.

I have the courage to walk away,

From a man who's never making me his, come

what may.

A. N. Gibbs

My Friend

A Smile That Radiates

My curves may not be ample,

But my smile, it shines so bright.

When I gaze upon your face,

It grows wider, day and night.

Words fail me sometimes,

For your presence takes my breath.

Your charm, it overwhelms,

As you fill my heart with grace.

On days when shadows creep,

And my spirit sinks so low,

You appear with open arms,

And banish all my woe.

Together, we bask in joy,

While youth's flame burns bright.

[101]

May our friendship never wane,
A beacon of love's light.

Though my butt may not be grand,
My smile, it radiates your worth.
In your embrace, I find my home,
A haven on this earthly earth.
A. N. Gibbs

Dream Come True

Love's Embrace

Amidst life's turmoil, where tensions rise,

You bring me solace, a calming breeze.

When I seek comfort,

in your arms I find release,

A sanctuary where worries cease.

Through countless years, our love has grown,

A tapestry of joy, a love profound.

Your presence sets my heart aflame,

A beacon of affection, a cherished name.

For all the ways you fill my days with grace,

I'd sing your praises for endless days.

Your love, a beacon,

guiding me through the night,

A dream come true, a heart's pure delight.

From mountaintops, I'll shout my love so bold,

For in your embrace, my story is told.

You are my everything, my guiding star,

My dream come true, my love from afar.

A. N. Gibbs

Don't

Love's Pavilion

Oh, love, a sacred sanctuary,

A haven where hearts find their sanctuary.

But beware, its walls can be fragile and thin,

If we tread carelessly, we may let sorrow in.

Like a delicate flower, it needs nurturing care,

Words and actions that heal, not tear.

Forgiveness may mend the broken, it's true,

But scars may linger,

a reminder of what we do.

Love yourself, as you would your own heart,

Respect the boundaries, play a fair part.

Let not your emotions

cloud your judgment's sight,

For actions taken in anger

can lead to a bitter fight.

Love is not a battlefield, where battles rage,

But a tranquil pavilion, where souls engage.

Its strength lies not in conquest or might,
But in the gentle embrace of day and night.

So let us tread softly, with hearts full of grace,
Preserving love's sanctuary, its sacred space.
For in its embrace, we find true bliss,
A symphony of souls, a tender kiss.
A. N. Gibbs

Tired

Tired of Being Second

My heart, a weary soul, no longer yearns,

To be a footnote, a mere shadow's turns.

I've shed my tears, faced every haunting fear,

But now, my love, it's time to make things clear.

I'm tired of being second, tired of less,

Of settling for crumbs, a love that's a mess.

I deserve more than scraps, a love that's true,

A bond that sets my soul aflame,

just me and you.

So please, my dear, understand my plea,

I'm weary of this dance, this endless misery.

I'm leaving now, my heart no longer bound,

To a love that's fractured, where I'm not found.

I'm tired of being second, tired of pain,

It's time to break the chains, to start again.

I'll find a love that's whole, a love that's pure,

Where I'm cherished, valued, and forever
secure.
A. N. Gibbs

My Apology

A Love Poem

In my expectant heart, you found your place,

A solace in the depths of sorrow's embrace.

When sadness whispered,

you became my guide,

Your presence a beacon in the stormy tide.

Your ears inclined to hear my every plea,

A patient listener, setting my spirit free.

In moments of anger, you remained my friend,

Understanding my wrath, until the bitter end.

Alone and desolate, I yearned for your sight,

A beacon of hope, dispelling the darkest night.

Your absence felt like a void I couldn't bear,

A constant ache, a longing beyond compare.

Demanding yet demanding, I held you tight,

Exhausted by my need,

I saw the weight of my plight.

I sought your constant presence,

a slave to my desire,

Ignoring the toll it took on your heart and fire.

Like a newborn babe, I cried for sustenance,

Expecting you to feed my soul's persistence.

But in my selfish ways, I failed to see,

The burden I placed upon you, unknowingly.

So now, with heavy heart and trembling hand,

I offer my apology, a promise to withstand.

No longer will I cling to you with such might,

For I have learned to stand on my own,

in the light.

Though the path ahead may still be fraught

with pain,

I will embrace the journey, with newfound

strength to gain.

Your love will always hold a special place,

But I will learn to love myself, with equal grace.

A. N. Gibbs

Soulmates

Love's Symphony

Our hearts entwined, a bond so deep,
Never neglected, our love we keep.
In sync we dance, our spirits bright,
United in dreams, a radiant light.

True love's embrace, a gentle sway,
Affection blooms, each passing day.
Like peanut butter and jelly, we're paired,
A perfect blend, our souls ensnared.

Butterflies flutter, a sweet delight,
In your presence, my heart takes flight.
We're intertwined, each other's guide,
Growing together, side by side.

Our thoughts and feelings, we share with care,
Keeping it real, our love we declare.

Honesty shines, a beacon so true,
Guiding our path, making dreams come true.

In this symphony of love, we find,
A connection that forever binds.
Through life's adventures, we'll stand as one,
Our love's melody, forever sung.
A. N. Gibbs

The Way

(The Nikki Gibbs Experience)

Captured Heart

With lightning speed, you seized my soul,

A captive of your charm, I'm now made whole.

Unfolding tales, no matter their guise,

You'll forever hold my heart, the prize.

Your smile, a beacon, bright and clear,

Ignites a flame that banishes fear.

At every hour, my thoughts take flight,

Engulfed in you, day and night.

My words falter, unable to convey

The depth of my desire, come what may.

With every moment spent in your embrace,

Love's promise blooms, a radiant grace.

My skies once gray now dance with blue,

All thanks to you, my love, it's true.

E. Wisemon

You could never be upset with the people who forced you into your dream or up higher.

~ Tyler Perry~

$\mathcal{M}e$

Nik's life was a battlefield filled with trials and losses, yet she stood tall with unwavering faith in God. Her heart remained kind despite the hardships she faced. She devoted herself to serving the community through volunteering at various organizations like American Legion Post 34, Kingdom Group Corporation, Inc, and Alpha Alpha Gamma Psi Christian Sorority Inc.

Her days were filled with selfless acts of kindness, bringing light to those in darkness. Nik found solace in being a beacon of hope for others. Despite the demands of her busy schedule, she never felt overwhelmed. In fact, helping others brought her immense joy and fulfillment.

Through her experiences, Nik learned the importance of self-care. She understood that to continue making a difference, she needed to prioritize her own well-being. It was a challenging lesson that shaped her into a stronger, more resilient individual.

Today, Nik stands as a symbol of hope and positivity in her community. Her life serves as a testament to the power of faith, resilience, and grace. She continues to thank God for guiding her through the darkest moments and leading her to a place of light and gratitude. Nik's story inspires others to find gratitude during adversity, showing that there is always a reason to be thankful.